THE UNAUTHORIZED
Court of Cocktails

THE UNAUTHORIZED
Court
of Cocktails

RECIPES FOR YOUR
ROMANTASIES

REYNA EDMONDS

This book has not been authorized, approved, licensed,
or endorsed by Sarah J. Maas, her publishers or licensees,
or any other author of a romantasy.

Countryman Press
An Imprint of W. W. Norton & Company
Independent Publishers Since 1923

This cocktail book is dedicated to my friends and family. To my incredible husband and children, thank you for supporting my aspirations and allowing me to pursue my passion. To my friends and family, thank you to everyone who helped me develop and taste cocktails and helped me create the beauty that lies in this book. To my mother-in-law for the countless hours spent perfecting the Australian sausage roll recipe with our American ingredients and letting me share it in this book, thank you! Finally, to Meg, Jess, and Carrie, thank you for introducing me to romantasy and helping create the magic that is in these pages.

Cheers!

Note from the Author

Dear reader,

Welcome to *The Unauthorized Court of Cocktails*. You are likely familiar with the romantasy genre, which contains a dastardly evocative and addictive set of books that have increasingly taken readers by storm. They offer us a true escape, fulfilling any fantasies we might have about mystical realms and beautiful lovers. I simply can't get enough of these sexy stories full of lust and empowered women, and you'll frequently find me with my nose in the latest trending trilogy.

My first dive into the genre was through Sarah J. Maas's A Court of Thorns and Roses, a series that I couldn't put down and made me fall in love with romantic fantasy books. The series follows Feyre, a young woman who learns both the dangers and the beauties of leaving her comfort zone and entering a world of magic, faeries, royal courts, immortality, and, of course, *very* sexy men. As with any romantasy heroine, Feyre doesn't just survive—she thrives, quickly finding her place in the fae realm she once feared. Throughout her journey, she doesn't just discover the depths of her inner strength but also the kind of love she craves—and deserves—from a partner bold enough to keep up with her passion. This is what sets romantasy apart from the classic romance genre; romantasy protagonists, very often women, get to go on the epic hero's journey that is common in the fantasy genre. These dynamic women use spells, make potions, or ride on the backs of dragons, and at the same time, they live out storybook romances.

This cocktail book is inspired by A Court of Thorns and Roses and its romantasy brethren. It's my hope that the recipes and images you'll find in these pages evoke the beauty, the magic, and at times, the fear of Feyre's story and of other romantasies like hers. I've used glitter to arouse thoughts of shimmering night skies, deep red liquors to conjure the sultry and velvety feelings of romance, and smoky backgrounds to call forth the cloying closeness of magic and danger. The recipe headnotes are crafted to immerse you in a scene as you create these cocktails, inviting you to step into romantasy worlds and let your own fantasies take over. And for those die-hard fans of the author and her work, you may find a few fan easter eggs sprinkled throughout.

For some recipes, I have taken direct inspiration from characters or scenes in the Court of Thorns and Roses series; in these cases, you will find a citation leading you to the book and chapter from whence this inspiration came (and you *should* think of this as mandatory reading homework if you've not read A Court of Thorns and Roses.) The other recipes are meant to evoke general scenes of romantasy, from starry-eyed lovers and hard-fought battles to dazzling skyscapes and glitzy faerie parties.

This book is entirely unofficial and unauthorized; it has not been endorsed in any fashion by Sarah J. Maas or her publisher. I created all of these recipes and images on my own with her words in mind simply because I wanted to inhabit her world and other romantasy worlds a bit longer. And I hope that you, dear reader, will find these recipes inspire the same thoughts of wonder, daring, bravery, darkness, and lust that we've found within the pages of the books we love so dearly—but with a new twist: You get to make these marvelous daydreams with your own hands in your own kitchen.

Cheers and kisses!
Reyna Edmonds

Contents

A Court of Vodka

Golden Lady

Pear Martini

✦ Makes 1 drink ✦

A symphony of floral and fruity notes, this drink promises to catapult you beyond the mortal realm and into the cosmic expanse. Who better to serve this ethereal concoction than the High Lord himself? His voice, velvet and edged with secrets, whispers in your ear, "Hello, darling."

3 ounces pear vodka
1½ ounces St. Germaine Elderflower
  Liqueur
3 ounces fresh pear juice

1½ ounces Simple Syrup (page 136)
1½ ounces fresh lemon juice
1 pear slice for garnish
Edible gold leaf for garnish

1. Prepare a cocktail shaker by filling it with a generous amount of ice.

2. Add in the pear vodka, elderflower liqueur, pear juice, simple syrup, and zesty lemon juice.

3. Shake vigorously until perfectly blended and you sense a familiar bond forming.

4. Carefully pour the mixture into a martini glass and adorn the glass with a delicate slice of pear and edible gold leaf. Now give into your fate as you turn to your High Lord and breathe in his citrusy scent as he kneels before you.

Shadow Singer

Hazelnut Espresso Martini

✦ Makes 1 drink ✦

This cocktail beckons you into the depths of the night, where secrets whisper on the wind and spies may lurk in every shadow. At its heart lies the rich intensity of espresso, its bold flavor a tribute to the mysteries that lurk in the darkness. With each sip, you'll feel the pulse of the night coursing through you, awakening your senses to the hidden truths that lie beneath the surface. But the addition of hazelnut, like a set of beautiful hazel eyes, lends a decadent twist to this martini, infusing it with a nutty sweetness that lingers on the palate.

Inspired by *A Court of Mist and Fury* by Sarah J. Maas (Chapter 16)

2 shots espresso

2 ounces vodka

1½ ounces Frangelico (or any hazelnut liqueur)

1½ ounces coffee liqueur

½ ounce Simple Syrup (page 136)

Espresso beans for garnish

1. Begin by preparing 2 shots of espresso and letting them cool to room temperature.

2. Fill a cocktail shaker with ice cubes.

3. Add the vodka, Frangelico, cooled espresso, coffee liqueur, and simple syrup into the shaker.

4. Make sure to tightly close the lid of the shaker and vigorously shake the mixture for approximately 15 to 20 seconds to achieve the perfect chill.

5. Carefully strain the mixture into a martini glass that has been prechilled.

6. Allow your shadows to encompass the cocktail as you place it next to a Truth Teller and garnish with fragrant espresso beans.

Midnight Mule

Blueberry Mule

✦ Makes 1 drink ✦

This celestial elixir beckons you to gaze upon the night sky and marvel at the wonders that lie beyond. At its core lies the sweet tang of blueberries, reminiscent of the midnight hues that paint the heavens above. Each sip is a taste of the infinite possibilities that await those who dare to dream. Paired with the fiery kick of ginger beer, this Moscow Mule–inspired cocktail sparkles like the stars themselves, its effervescence a tribute to the shimmering constellations that adorn the night sky. With each sip, you'll feel the magic of the cosmos coursing through you, igniting your spirit with its celestial light.

½ cup fresh blueberries
2 ounces blueberry-infused vodka
    (see Infused Alcohol, page 140)
½ ounce fresh lime juice

4 to 6 ounces ginger beer
Fresh blueberries for garnish
Lime slices for garnish
Mint leaves for garnish (optional)

1. In a cocktail shaker, muddle the blueberries until they release their juices.

2. Add the vodka and lime juice to the shaker.

3. Fill the shaker with ice cubes.

4. Shake the mixture well until it's thoroughly chilled.

5. Fill a copper mug or glass with ice cubes.

6. Strain the blueberry vodka mixture into the mug or glass.

7. Top off with ginger beer, leaving some space at the top for garnish.

8. Stir gently to combine.

9. Garnish with fresh blueberries, lime slices, and mint leaves (if using) and sip as you witness a spinning galaxy from within your glass.

Bat Boys

Blackberry Lime Cocktail

✦ Makes 1 drink ✦

This sensual cocktail will bend your mind, send a shadow tingling down your spine, and excite your senses as you sip. The sweet notes of blackberry and orange pair well with the tart burst of lime, making an irresistible melody of citrus notes. Consumer beware: This drink is known to give dreams of large, winged warriors ready to sweep you into a fantasy only stories are made of. Do you dare fly with these flavors?

Inspired by *A Court of Mist and Fury* by Sarah J. Maas (Chapter 7)

2 ounces Blackberry Liqueur
  (page 139)
1 ounce vodka
1 teaspoon fresh lime juice
1 teaspoon Simple Syrup (page 136)

½ teaspoon activated charcoal
Dash of orange bitters
Ginger beer (optional)
1 blackberry for garnish
Rosemary sprig for garnish

1. Combine all the ingredients except the ginger beer and garnishes in a shaker and give it a vigorous shake, allowing their flavors to intertwine in a harmonious dance.

2. Gently pour into a glass over ice.

3. For those seeking a touch of effervescence, crown this masterpiece with the embrace of ginger beer, adding a playful sparkle to your senses.

4. To elevate this creation to a level of sheer opulence, adorn it with the regal presence of a succulent blackberry and a fragrant sprig of rosemary, transforming it into a work of art that tantalizes both the eyes and the palate.

Tiny Ancient One

Vodka Pomegranate Fizz

✦ Makes 1 drink ✦

The deep crimson hue of pomegranate juice forms the heart of this cocktail, symbolizing the ancient creatures of the realm who are sustained by blood. Each sip is a journey through ancient realms, with the tartness of lime adding a sharp, invigorating twist. This drink mirrors the Tiny Ancient One's fierce and unyielding nature. Known as a powerful messenger and assassin for a wrathful god, this is a being you do not want to cross. As you raise your glass to the Tiny Ancient One, let the flavors transport you to another universe where ancient power and modern grace intertwine.

Inspired by *A Court of Mist and Fury* by Sarah J. Maas (Chapter 14)

2 ounces premium vodka
1 ounce pomegranate juice
½ ounce fresh lime juice
½ ounce Simple Syrup (page 136)

Club soda or sparkling water
Pomegranate seeds for garnish
Lime wheel for garnish

1. Blend together the vodka, luscious pomegranate juice, zesty lime juice, and simple syrup in an elegant shaker.

2. Add a generous amount of ice to the shaker and shake with finesse for approximately 15 seconds.

3. Carefully strain the mixture into a glass already filled with ice cubes.

4. Elevate the drink by pouring in club soda.

5. Gently mix the components together with a sophisticated stir.

6. Adorn the beverage with a sprinkle of pomegranate seeds and a lime wheel for a touch of extravagence.

Bloody Battle

Garlic Bloody Mary

✦ Makes 1 drink ✦

Whether you are recovering from a night out at the dance hall or trying to heal from going to war, this cocktail is sure to cure any ailment. At its heart, the Bloody Battle features the robust flavors of tomato juice, and the infusion of garlic adds a powerful, savory punch that will surely give you the confidence of a warrior. As you raise your glass of Bloody Battle, let the flavors transport you to the heart of the fray or away from any porcelain gods.

Celery salt
1 lemon wedge
1 lime wedge
2 ounces garlic-infused vodka
  (see Infused Alcohol, page 140)
Mr. & Mrs. T Bloody Mary Mix
2 teaspoons prepared horseradish

2 dashes Tabasco sauce
2 dashes Worcestershire sauce
Dash of lemon pepper
Pickles, bacon, pickled asparagus,
  green olives, lime slice, and/or stalk
  of celery for garnish

1. Sprinkle a bit of celery salt onto a small plate.

2. Gently rub the succulent side of the lemon or lime slice along the rim of a pint glass.

3. Roll the outer edge of the glass in the celery salt until it is completely coated, then fill the glass with ice.

4. Squeeze the lemon and lime slices into the glass.

5. Pour the vodka, Bloody Mary mix, horseradish, Tabasco, Worcestershire sauce, lemon pepper, and a dash of celery salt into the glass and stir.

6. Decorate with a medley of pickles, bacon, pickled asparagus, two speared green olives, a lime slice, and a stalk of celery.

Witch's Ember

Flaming Lemon Drop

✦ **Makes 3 shots** ✦

Ignite your senses with the Witch's Ember, a tart and fiery lemon drop shot that captures the intense passion and searing journey between a hot-tempered witch and a noble soldier. The sharpness of the fresh lemon juice reflects the fierce and unyielding spirits of two stubborn lovers. Feel the burn of their struggles and the warmth of their triumphs, savoring each moment of their journey toward acceptance and healing. Embrace the fire within and let it light the way through the darkness.

1 lemon	1 ounce Simple Syrup (page 136)
2½ ounces citron vodka	1 teaspoon sugar
1 ounce fresh lemon juice	¼ teaspoon 151 rum

1. Slice the lemon into ¼-inch rounds; set aside.

2. Fill a cocktail shaker with ice.

3. Pour the citron vodka, lemon juice, and simple syrup into the cocktail shaker.

4. Shake and strain into three shot glasses.

5. Place one lemon slice flat on the top rim of each shot glass and pour some sugar on top toward the center of the lemon.

6. Pour 151 rum onto the sugar on each lemon, ensuring the sugar absorbs it.

7. Light the sugar and rum with a lighter and watch the flames dance.

8. Let the flame completely die out before removing the lemon and taking the shot.

Frosted Fizz

Berry Vodka Cocktail

✦ Makes 1 drink ✦

In the Frosted Fizz, frost-kissed cranberries evoke the icy landscapes of a winter wonderland. Paired with the crisp bite of vodka, each sip fills you with a chilling intrigue. But it's the sprig of rosemary that adds an unexpected twist, infusing the cocktail with a whisper of earthy warmth amid the frost.

½ ounce lime-infused simple syrup
   (see Simple Syrup, page 136)
Rosemary sprig

Edible glitter
1½ ounces premium vodka
Cranberry or berry hard seltzer

1. Begin by delicately pouring the lime-infused simple syrup into an elegant champagne flute or wine glass.

2. Place the rosemary sprig upside down in the glass, allowing it to gracefully soak in the sweet syrup.

3. Place the flute in the freezer until the syrup is frozen, creating a stunning visual of the rosemary standing tall like a majestic tree.

4. Sprinkle a touch of edible glitter into the flute for a touch of glamour.

5. Carefully pour the vodka into the flute, adding a touch of sophistication.

6. Lastly, pour the hard seltzer on top with the utmost care, filling the glass with effervescence and luxury.

Death Kiss

Chocolate Raspberry Martini

✦ Makes 1 drink ✦

Indulge in this exquisite chocolate martini after a thrilling escape from the clutches of a goddess of death. It is not unusual to find this death god weaving the hair of her defeated foes, and those who manage to survive her deadly embrace deserve a treat for their valor. Despite her aged and haggard visage, she can transform into a vision of wrath and allure, much like the transformation one experiences with just a single taste of this velvety drink.

1½ ounces milk chocolate liqueur
1 ounce crème de cacao
1 ounce raspberry vodka

3 ounces half-and-half
1 fresh raspberry or chocolate shaving
   for garnish (optional)

1. Place a martini glass in the freezer for a few minutes to chill.

2. Fill your cocktail shaker halfway with ice.

3. Pour in the milk chocolate liqueur, letting the rich, chocolatey goodness flow in.

4. Add the crème de cacao, enhancing the chocolate depth.

5. Include the raspberry vodka, introducing a fruity elegance.

6. Finally, pour in the half-and-half for a creamy, smooth texture.

7. Secure the lid on your shaker and shake vigorously for 15 to 20 seconds, until the mixture is well chilled and frothy.

8. Remove the chilled martini glass from the freezer.

9. Strain the luscious mixture into the glass, allowing the creamy chocolate-raspberry martini to fill it.

10. For an extra touch of elegance, garnish with a raspberry or a chocolate shaving on the rim.

Dread Trove

Cinnamon Butterscotch Martini

✦ Makes 1 drink ✦

This spectacular concoction exudes an aura of unparalleled grandeur for anyone fortunate enough to revel in its splendor. Commencing with the resplendent glimmer of Goldschläger, this drink evokes images of regal crowns that once a majestic queen. The velvety caress of Baileys Irish Cream possesses the ability to beckon forth spirits from realms beyond our own. With each sip, the delectable essence of butterscotch dances upon the palate like the gentle strumming of a harp. And finally, the enigmatic and opulent flavor of Jägermeister, though concealed, is an indispensable component. Each sip serves as a poignant reminder of the extravagant opulence and lavishness of a maker's craftsmanship, bestowing upon its imbiber a taste of enchantment and boundless power.

Inspired by *A Court of Silver Flames* by Sarah J. Maas (Chapter 21)

½ ounce Goldschläger
½ ounce Baileys Irish Cream
½ ounce butterscotch schnapps

½ ounce Jägermeister
Gold edible glitter

1. Begin by chilling a martini glass to cold perfection.

2. Pour in the velvety blend of Goldschläger, Baileys Irish Cream, butterscotch schnapps, and Jägermeister over ice in a cocktail shaker.

3. Sprinkle in the shimmering gold edible glitter for an extra touch of glamour.

4. Shake the concoction vigorously to meld all the lavish flavors.

5. Remember to add ice and gently stir before indulging in this decadent libation. Serve your impeccably crafted drink promptly, savoring the harmonious interplay of colors and textures.

Under the Mountain

Raspberry Pomegranate Martini

✦ Makes 1 drink ✦

Step into the mysterious abyss of a malevolent raspberry, pomegranate, and lime martini. Within its depths lies a crimson hue, a chilling reminder of the bloodshed that stained the land during the reign of a powerful queen. With each sip, the lime's tang cuts through, leaving an unyielding bitterness that echoes her merciless deeds.

This bewitching concoction mirrors her beguiling allure, concealing layers of wickedness beneath her enchanting facade. As you raise your glass to your fallen friends, allow the flavors to transport you to a realm where every shadow holds a new torment and every taste is accompanied by the eerie sensation of being watched. Embrace the darkness and never forget the consequences of crossing paths with such a formidable adversary.

Inspired by *A Court of Thorns and Roses* by Sarah J. Maas (Chapter 33)

3 ounces raspberry vodka	**2 ounces pomegranate juice**
1 ounce premium raspberry liqueur	**1 ounce fresh lime juice**

1. Chill a martini glass so it's as cold as the queen's heart.

2. Fill your finest cocktail shaker with ice. Add elegance by pouring in the raspberry vodka.

3. Add the raspberry liqueur, its opulent, deep red hue enhancing the blend with notes of fear and torture.

4. Incorporate the ruby tones of pure pomegranate juice for refined sweetness.

5. Delicately add the lime juice for a fresh, vibrant edge.

6. Shake viciously to make the High Lords tremble in your presence.

7. Strain this concoction into your chilled martini glass.

Starlit Gaze

Purple Citrus Vodka Martini

✦ Makes 1 drink ✦

As you sip this cocktail it will feel as though you are gazing into the sparkling eyes of an enemy-turned-lover. Savor the citrus scent of the vodka while mixing the deep purple hue of the blue curaçao combined with the grenadine, which mirrors the enigmatic depths of his gaze, while the fresh lime juice and limeade add a tantalizing balance of tart and sweet, much like the irresistible charm that draws you in. As you sip, the silver glitter swirls in the glass, creating a celestial dance that captures the essence of his otherworldly beauty and magnetic presence.

2 ounces citrus vodka
1 ounce blue curaçao
½ ounce grenadine
½ ounce fresh lime juice

2 ounces limeade or lemonade
Pinch of silver edible glitter plus more
for serving

1. Chill a coupe or martini glass until it's perfectly frosty.

2. In a cocktail shaker filled with ice, combine the vodka, blue curaçao, grenadine, lime juice, limeade, and edible glitter.

3. Vigorously shake the mixture for about 20 seconds, blending the flavors and chilling the drink to perfection.

4. Strain the seductive purple elixir into your chilled glass, allowing its vibrant color to captivate at first sight.

5. Finish with another delicate sprinkle of edible glitter, imbuing the drink with a celestial shimmer reminiscent of a starlit lover's gaze.

A Court
of Rum

Crimson Veil

Black Cherry and Rum Martini

✦ Makes 1 drink ✦

Dark cherry juice forms the heart of this cocktail, its deep crimson hue reminiscent of the blood spilled and the passions ignited within royal faerie courts. Each sip is a reminder of the forbidden desires and dangerous liaisons that pulse beyond the walls of a glittering facade. The addition of peach schnapps lends a delicate sweetness to the drink, evoking the heady aroma of summer blossoms and the intoxicating allure of love. But it's the rum that adds a fiery edge, infusing the cocktail with a boldness and depth that mirrors the untamed spirit of the characters and creatures who inhabit a magical world.

2 ounces white rum
½ ounce peach schnapps
3 ounces black cherry juice
½ ounce fresh lime juice

2 teaspoons grenadine
Rose stem with thorns for garnish
 (optional)

1. Combine the seductive flavors of rum, peach schnapps, black cherry juice, lime juice, and grenadine in a tantalizing dance within the confines of a cocktail shaker, surrounded by a bed of ice.

2. Shake with passion for a mere 10 seconds, allowing the ingredients to intertwine and embrace, creating a harmonious symphony of flavors that will send shivers down your spine.

3. Gently pour this elixir of desire into a martini glass, straining out any remnants of ice, and prepare to fall into a sensory journey that will leave you craving more.

4. Garnish with a rose stem if you are feeling venturesome.

Summer Solstice

Rum and Passion Fruit Cocktail

✦ Makes 1 drink ✦

Embrace the harmonious blend of rum, passion fruit, and lime that encapsulates the magic of faerie festivities during the solstice. Embrace the balance of day and night with this libation, allowing yourself to be swept away in the jubilant spirit of the season. With a splash of bubbles, this cocktail shimmers with lively vigor, reminiscent of the bonfires that light up the night and the cheerful melodies that echo through the air. Each sip will awaken your senses to the boundless opportunities that lie ahead, filling you with the essence of the season. Cheers to the solstice, a time for dancing, excessive drinking, and dallying in the whimsy of faerie delight.

2 ounces light rum
½ ounce fresh lime juice

1 ounce passion fruit puree or syrup
3 ounces sparkling wine or champagne

1. Start by filling a cocktail shaker with ice. Proceed to add the rum, lime juice, and passion fruit puree.

2. Ensure the shaker lid is securely closed, then shake vigorously.

3. Strain the mixture into a martini glass and finish it off by topping it with the sparkling wine.

4. Now it's time to serve and savor this delightful concoction!

Royal Tides

Dark and Stormy

✦ Makes 1 drink ✦

Just as the Summer Court's cities exude elegance and grace, this libation combines the rich flavors of dark rum and ginger beer to create a drink that is as enchanting as it is exhilarating. At its heart lies the deep, complex notes of dark rum, evoking the regal splendor of the Summer Court's mountain-island palace. Each sip is a journey through the swirling mists and rolling waves of the sea, where the intensity of the rum ignites the senses and sets the stage for an unforgettable adventure.

Inspired by *A Court of Mist and Fury* by Sarah J. Maas (Chapter 32)

3 ounces chilled ginger beer
½ ounce fresh lime juice

2 ounces dark rum
Lime wheel

1. Fill a highball glass with glistening ice. Add the ginger beer and the delicate splash of lime juice.

2. Introduce the floater of rich dark rum, allowing it to gracefully mingle with the refreshing concoction below.

3. As a final touch of opulence, adorn this masterpiece with a vibrant lime wheel, adding a burst of citrusy allure to the already captivating presentation.

Firefae Punch

Apple Cider Rum Punch

✦ Makes 1 drink ✦

Revel in this apple cider punch, a luxurious cocktail crafted to embody the fine allure and powerful essence of autumn. At its core lies the warm, spiced notes of apple cider, a tribute to the lush and vibrant woods that resemble a jeweled mosaic. Each sip is a walk through the forest, where the crisp air is filled with the scent of autumn leaves and the promise of adventure. The addition of spiced rum echoes the bite of autumn's dark nights, igniting the senses and adding a touch of intrigue to the punch.

Caramel sauce
Raw sugar or cinnamon sugar
½ cup apple cider
2 ounces spiced rum
1 tablespoon maple syrup

2 apple slices, ¼ inch thick
Cinnamon stick
1 teaspoon granulated sugar
½ teaspoon cinnamon
1 teaspoon 151 rum

1. Immerse the edge of your elegant glass in luscious caramel sauce followed by a delicate coating of raw sugar.

2. Allow the glass to cool in the refrigerator.

3. Add a touch of sophistication by combining the apple cider, spiced rum, and rich maple syrup in a shaker filled with ice.

4. Carefully pour the decadent mixture into your chilled glass and adorn with one of the crisp apple slices and a fragrant cinnamon stick.

5. Mix the sugar and cinnamon together.

6. Place the second apple slice on top of the glass, pour the cinnamon sugar onto the center of the apple and then pour the rum onto the cinnamon sugar.

7. Carefully hold a lighter to the rum and sugar until they catch alight.

8. Wait until the flame is gone to consume the cocktail.

Blood Rite

Blood Orange and Cranberry Mojito

✦ Makes 1 drink ✦

Experience a dynamic fusion that reflects the intense challenges and primal battles of an annual ritual in the Illyrian Mountains. This drink honors the perseverance, grit, and survival instincts of young warriors as they brave dangerous terrain and confront daunting obstacles to prove their mettle.

At its essence, the tangy sweetness of blood orange symbolizes the familial bonds and connections that bind people together. Each sip takes you on a voyage through the rugged mountain landscape, where the zesty citrus notes awaken the spirit and strengthen the soul against the unforgiving elements. Raise your glass to the Blood Rite and let the flavors transport you to the core of the mountains, where every sip is a tribute to the unyielding spirit and resolute determination of the warriors who choose to attempt this dangerous ceremony.

Inspired by *A Court of Silver Flames* by Sarah J. Maas (Chapter 66)

3 or 4 mint leaves, more for garnish
2 ounces white rum
4 ounces unsweetened pure
   cranberry juice

1 ounce fresh lime juice
Blood orange soda
Lime wedges and fresh mint
   for garnish

1. In a shaker, muddle the mint leaves. Add the white rum, cranberry juice, and lime juice to the shaker with the muddled mint.

2. Fill the shaker with ice, then shake well until the mixture is chilled (15 to 20 seconds).

3. Fill a large cocktail glass with ice and pour in the mixed cocktail.

4. Top off the drink with the blood orange soda, adding it slowly to avoid overflowing.

5. Garnish with fresh mint and lime.

White Wedding

Coconut Rum Martini

✦ Makes 1 drink ✦

This cocktail captures the tension and beauty of a fated moment, blending elements of elegance, panic, and unexpected rescue into a drink that is as complex and compelling as the scene it represents. The smoothness of rum sets a sophisticated foundation, echoing the ornate and meticulously planned wedding that a young human finds herself in. The addition of coconut introduces a creamy, tropical note, symbolizing the layers of tradition and expectation that weigh heavily on her. The sweet pop of rose may trigger your senses, as it triggered the young human's desire to be saved, and spark a flame that may lead you down a midnight path . . .

Inspired by *A Court of Mist and Fury* by Sarah J. Maas (Chapter 5)

2 ounces unflavored coconut milk
2 ounces white rum
½ ounce Malibu liqueur

1 teaspoon rose simple syrup
(see Simple Syrup, page 136)
1 rose for garnish

1. Incorporate the velvety essence of coconut milk, the refined notes of white rum, the exotic allure of Malibu, and the delicate sweetness of rose simple syrup into your elegant cocktail shaker.

2. Introduce a generous handful of ice into your shaker, allowing it to embrace the ingredients with a refreshing chill.

3. Engage in a spirited dance of flavors as you vigorously shake the concoction, ensuring a harmonious fusion of all its elements. Then, with grace and finesse, pour the elixir into a glass that has been patiently awaiting its arrival in a state of chilled anticipation.

4. Elevate the presentation of this opulent libation by adorning it with a garnish of delicate rose petals or a single bud, adding a touch of sophistication and beauty to your already stunning creation.

Magic's Bane

Rum, Mint, and Champagne

✦ Makes 1 drink ✦

This elegant blend harmonizes the rich depth of rum, the invigorating zing of mint, and the subtle allure of simple syrup, all enhanced by the sparkling allure of champagne. This magical elixir may just be able to subdue the most powerful in the realm with a single sip. Magic's Bane is a beverage that captivates the palate and lingers in memory. But beware, fair warrior: Too many sips of this drink may leave you powerless . . .

2 mint leaves
2 ounces dark spiced rum
1 ounce fresh lime juice
1 ounce brown sugar simple syrup
   (see Simple Syrup, page 136)

Champagne or sparkling wine to
   fill glass
Mint sprig or lime peel for garnish

1. Chill a large wine glass or a coupe to ensure it's perfectly frosty.

2. In a cocktail shaker, gently muddle the mint leaves to release their fragrant oils.

3. Add the dark spiced rum, lime juice, and brown sugar simple syrup to the shaker with the muddled mint. Fill the shaker with ice.

4. Vigorously shake the mixture for 15 to 20 seconds to blend the flavors and chill the drink thoroughly.

5. Strain the mixture into your chilled glass, filling it about two-thirds full.

6. Carefully top off the cocktail with champagne, letting it bubble and effervesce as it mingles with the dark, spiced base.

7. Garnish with a sprig of fresh mint or a twist of lime peel for an added touch of elegance.

A Court of Whiskey

Lord of Bastards

Smoked Rosemary Old-Fashioned

✦ Makes 1 drink ✦

A lord of bastards unveils his clandestine concoction. A tumbler of whiskey, aged in oak barrels as ancient as his vendettas, mirrors the hue of his resplendent golden eyes. Accompanied by the fragrant essence of smoldering rosemary, this combination accentuates the unwavering loyalty of a formidable warrior. Despite being dreaded by many, it is he who craves this potent libation after a day in the sparring ring with the realm's chosen hero.

Inspired by *A Court of Wings and Ruin* by Sarah J. Maas (Chapter 22)

For the Smoked Rosemary
2 to 3 smoked rosemary sprigs
    (steps to follow)
Culinary torch

For the Old-Fashioned
2 ounces Irish whiskey
½ ounce honey ginger simple syrup
    (see Simple Syrup, page 136)
2 dashes Angostura bitters
2 dashes orange bitters
1 orange peel twist for garnish
Rosemary sprig for garnish

TO SMOKE THE ROSEMARY

1. Cut the rosemary into small pieces and place them on a wooden cutting board or heat-safe surface.

2. Use a culinary torch to light the rosemary on fire. Allow the flames to die down until you're left with smoldering rosemary.

3. Place a double old-fashioned glass upside down on top of the rosemary and let the smoke infuse the glass while preparing your cocktail.

continues

TO CONCOCT THE DRINK

1. Combine the Irish whiskey, honey ginger syrup, Angostura bitters, and orange bitters in a mixing glass, allowing their flavors to intertwine sensually.

2. Embrace the mixing glass with ice cubes, gently stirring to create a harmonious blend.

3. Pour the luscious concoction into the smoked double old-fashioned glass, straining it over a magnificent ice cube.

4. Unleash the tantalizing aroma of the orange peel as its zest dances gracefully over the cocktail, adorning it with elegance alongside a delicate sprig of rosemary.

Day Court

Honey Ginger Whiskey Sour

✦ Makes 1 drink ✦

This smooth libation is a testament to the court's illustrious heritage of safeguarding wisdom and cultivating ingenuity. Nestled at its core is the comforting embrace of ginger, its tantalizing nuances paying homage to the Day Court's insatiable thirst for exploration and innovation. With every sip, one embarks on a captivating odyssey through the hallowed halls of knowledge as the fiery ginger enlivens the senses and ignites the spark of imagination.

Inspired by *A Court of Thorns and Roses* by Sarah J. Maas (Chapter 45)

¾ ounce honey ginger simple syrup
   (see Simple Syrup, page 136)
2 ounces Jameson whiskey or other
   Irish whiskey

¾ ounce fresh lemon juice
Edible gold leaf garnish

1. Craft the enchanting honey ginger simple syrup.

2. Combine the syrup, whiskey, and lemon juice within a shaker, accompanied by a touch of ice.

3. Vigorously shake this concoction and gracefully strain it into a glass, where a magnificent ice cube awaits.

4. Embellish this elixir with a delicate gold leaf, adding a touch of enchantment to its appearance.

Into Darkness

Blackberry Whiskey Smash

✦ **Makes 1 drink** ✦

Give in to the essence of a formidable faerie lord with this exquisite cocktail. The artful combination of bold flavors and a hint of dark sophistication captures the allure and mystery that surrounds him. At its core, the deep and velvety bourbon notes embody his commanding presence and the smoky allure of his immense power. To mirror a dark lord's sensual charm and captivating beauty, fresh blackberries are added, infusing a dark and luscious sweetness. Just like his effortless grace, the mint's coolness and the lemon's tartness create a perfect harmony, striking a balance between charm and danger. Each moment spent embracing its flavors is a testament to his unrivaled magnificence.

Granulated sugar
Zest from 1 lime
Lime wedge
8 fresh blackberries
7 mint leaves, more for garnish

Juice from ½ lemon
1 tablespoon honey
2 ounces bourbon
Ginger beer

1. Combine the sugar and lime zest on a shallow plate. Glide a lime wedge along the rim of your glass, then flip the glass onto the plate to form a delightful sugar and lime rim.

2. Place the blackberries, mint, lemon juice, and honey in a cocktail shaker or glass jar. With a muddler, mix all the ingredients together, pressing everything to release the luscious juices, and then pour in the bourbon.

3. Fill your rimmed glass with ice and carefully pour the drink over the ice.

4. Add a bit more ice to the glass and pour the ginger beer over it, gently stirring to blend everything together.

5. Finish off with a touch of fresh mint.

Wingspan

Cold Brew and Bourbon

✦ Makes 1 drink ✦

This well-crafted libation is most delightfully savored following the spectacle of three valiant warriors engaging in a playful skirmish with snowballs, reminiscent of their carefree childhood days. In this enchanting moment, where sorcery is held at bay and the grace of flight is temporarily relinquished, the victor shall be determined by the sole warrior who remains unscathed by the icy grip of frostbite. As a discerning lady of intellect, it is only fitting that you gracefully await the conclusion of this battle, drinking in this wickedly delightful toasted concoction. And as the final snowball is hurled through the air, these gallant warriors may proudly display their majestic wingspan, for it is said that the grandeur of their wings is directly proportional to the magnificence of . . . other body parts.

Inspired by *A Court of Frost and Starlight* by Sarah J. Maas (Chapter 18)

1½ ounces fine bourbon
2 ounces rich cold brew coffee
¼ ounce fresh orange juice

½ ounce amaretto
1 marshmallow for garnish

1. Blend together the bourbon, coffee, zesty orange juice, and divine amaretto in a shaker of opulence.

2. Add in ice to chill to perfection.

3. Vigorously shake the concoction and strain it into a grand rocks glass. Skewer a decadent marshmallow on a bamboo spear or a cocktail pick.

4. Toast the marshmallow to a golden hue and elegantly garnish your delicious drink.

Captive Flame

Hard Apple Cider and Fireball

✦ Makes 1 drink ✦

This cocktail embodies the scorching intensity of a captive fae's anguish, the unwavering fortitude that courses through his veins, and the intricate depths of a man subjected to the shackles of servitude. Nestled at its very essence, the robust apple cider provides a tantalizingly crisp and invigorating foundation. Each sip is a reminder of the fresh beginnings a prisoner longs for, the sweetness of freedom just out of reach.

2 ounces Fireball Whisky
½ ounce fresh lime juice

Hard dry apple cider

1. Imbue a crystal-clear glass vessel with a cascade of pristine ice cubes, each one glistening like a precious gem.

2. Infuse the chilled elixir with the fiery essence of Fireball, a tantalizing blend of cinnamon and spice, and the splash of zesty lime, adding a vibrant twist to the concoction.

3. Crown this masterpiece with the effervescent nectar of a dry, hard apple cider, allowing its crisp and refreshing notes to dance upon your palate, creating a symphony of flavors that will transport you to a realm of pure luxury and indulgence.

A Court
of Gin

Spring Court

French 75

✦ Makes 1 drink ✦

At this drink's heart lies the floral aroma of lavender, evoking the fragrant fields that burst into bloom with the arrival of spring. Each sip is a journey through a sprawling manor and a reminder of the promise of new beginnings and endless possibilities. Paired with the effervescence of champagne, this cocktail sparkles like the sunlight dancing on freshly bloomed flowers, its bubbles a celebration of life and renewal. Drinking the Spring Court, you'll feel the warmth of the sun on your skin and the gentle breeze of springtime caressing your senses.

Inspired by *A Court of Thorns and Roses* by Sarah J. Maas (Chapter 6)

2 ounces Empress 1908 Indigo Gin
½ ounce orange liqueur
1 ounce fresh lemon juice
1 ounce lavender simple syrup
   (see Simple Syrup, page 136)

2 ounces champagne or sparkling wine
Lemon twist for garnish
Sprinkle of lavender for garnish

1. Incorporate the essence of gin, orange liqueur, lemon juice, and lavender simple syrup into a refined cocktail shaker with ice.

2. Vigorously shake the concoction, allowing the flavors to intertwine harmoniously.

3. Gracefully strain the resulting elixir into a coupe glass, elevating its presentation.

4. Top with champagne.

5. Adorn this masterpiece with a delicate lemon twist and a sprinkle of lavender, enhancing its allure and captivating the senses.

Winter Court

Gin Silver Fizz

✦ Makes 1 pitcher ✦

Slip into winter with this frozen mix in which the crisp and botanical notes of gin evoke the court's refined elegance. Each sip is a journey through snow-covered forests and grand, icy halls, where the spirit of the season is ever-present. Let the flavors transport you to a realm of luxurious palaces and roaring hearths, where reindeer-drawn sleighs glide over snow and white bears stand guard in the frosty wilderness.

Inspired by *A Court of Thorns and Roses* by Sarah J. Maas (Chapter 26)

6 to 8 ounces gin
3 heaping tablespoons frozen
   lemonade concentrate
2 heaping tablespoons frozen limeade
   concentrate

1 heaping tablespoon frozen orange
   juice concentrate
1 cup whole milk
2 cups crushed ice
Nutmeg for garnish

1. Combine all the ingredients except the nutmeg in a blender and blend until perfectly smooth.

2. Present this delightful concoction in an elegantly chilled glass.

3. Finish off this masterpiece by delicately sprinkling a touch of nutmeg for a flavorful garnish.

Flower Grower

Gin and Berry Spritz

✦ Makes 1 drink ✦

The Flower Grower emerges as a delicate elixir. Crafted from gin, botanical-infused syrup, and fresh berries, it whispers of dew-kissed petals and sun-drenched meadows. It is best to sip this decadent libation after a day laboring in the garden.

2 ounces gin
1 ounce rosemary simple syrup
   (see Simple Syrup, page 136)
Fresh raspberries and blackberries,
   more for garnish

1 rosemary sprig, more for garnish
½ lemon
½ lime
Plain sparkling water
Flowers for garnish

1. Combine the gin, simple syrup, fresh berries, and fragrant rosemary in a tall glass.

2. Gently crush and mix all the ingredients at the base of the glass and strain if desired.

3. Introduce some ice cubes with finesse.

4. Squeeze in the zesty essence of lemon and lime.

5. Crown this masterpiece with effervescent sparkling water.

6. Adorn the creation with delicate flowers, succulent berries, and aromatic rosemary sprigs.

Spill the Tea

Gin and Earl Grey Tea

✦ Makes 1 drink ✦

This drink compels only honest words to be spoken. Although the messenger of this warning may be elusive and intimidating in appearance, they carry messages through the woods for those who seek the truth.

6 ounces Earl Grey tea
2 ounces gin

1 ounce honey simple syrup
(see Simple Syrup, page 136)
1 ounce fresh lemon juice

1. Steep the Earl Grey tea, allowing its flavors to infuse for a minimum of 10 minutes.

2. Place ice into a shaker, chilling it to an icy coldness.

3. Combine all the ingredients within the shaker, blending their enigmatic essences.

4. Vigorously shake the concoction, as if stirring the truths you hold within.

5. Carefully strain the bewitching elixir into a glass, where a large, chilling cube of ice awaits its arrival.

Celestial Glimmer

Gin and Pear Cocktail

✦ Makes 1 drink ✦

This dazzling libation captures the essence of a magnificent mountain kingdom lit by the stars. This two-toned drink combines the regal flavors of Empress 1908 gin and crème de violette, accented with the delicate sweetness of pear and the fiery kick of ginger beer. Raise your glass to the starlit skies and the endless possibilities that await, as far-reaching as the sparkling heavens themselves.

3 ounces fresh pear juice
1 ounce fresh lemon juice
2 ounces ginger beer

2 ounces Empress 1908 Indigo Gin
1 ounce crème de violette
Edible star glitter garnish

1. Start by selecting a tall glass and filling it with ice cubes to chill it. This will ensure your cocktail stays refreshingly cold.

2. Pour the pear juice, lemon juice, and ginger beer into the bottom of the glass.

3. Add the Empress gin and crème de violette into a cocktail shaker of ice and shake to combine.

4. Carefully pour the Empress gin and crème de violette over the back of a spoon into the glass of pear juice, lemon juice, and ginger beer to create a layered effect, with the purple hue floating atop the golden drink.

5. Garnish your cocktail with a sprinkle of some edible glitter over the top to mimic the sparkle of a starlit sky.

Honesty Elixir

Cloudy Blue Cheese Martini

✦ Makes 1 drink ✦

Unveil the sharp edge of candor with the Honesty Elixir, a dirty martini with blue cheese that embodies a mystical ability to bring forth the truth. At its core, this martini is classic and uncompromising; the robust flavor of olive brine adds a salty depth, mirroring the drinker's inner desires. Delicious but dangerous, proceed with caution, as you never know what secrets you'll spill while sipping this savory concoction . . .

Splash of vermouth
3 ounces Bombay Sapphire gin
2½ ounces olive brine

Artisanal blue cheese
3 blue cheese–stuffed olives
    for garnish

1. Chill the martini glass for 10 minutes in the icy depths of the freezer.

2. Cleanse the glass with vermouth, rid it of the surplus, and return it to the frozen realm.

3. Within a shrouded cocktail shaker filled with ice, combine the gin, olive brine, and a chunk of blue cheese.

4. Extract the glass from its frosty slumber.

5. Vigorously shake the cocktail shaker 50 times and pour the concoction into the chilled martini glass.

6. Add blue cheese–stuffed olives for garnish.

7. Sip and enjoy as it assists you in discerning the truth of your foes.

Realm of Roses

Rose Gin and Honey Cocktail

✦ Makes 1 drink ✦

Crafted with the ethereal Empress 1908 Elderflower Rose Gin, this libation beckons with a floral elegance fit for faerie royalty. A harmonious blend of freshly squeezed lemon adds a zesty brightness, while a delicate touch of honey ginger simple syrup imbues a subtle warmth, reminiscent of the intricate layers of a mortal's evolving relationship with the fae. Sip slowly and let the flavors transport you to a realm where magic thrives and danger lurks in every shadow.

3 ounces Empress 1908 Elderflower Rose Gin
1 ounce fresh lemon juice

1 ounce honey ginger simple syrup (see Simple Syrup, page 136)
Champagne to top

1. Allow a coupe or martini glass to luxuriate in the frosty embrace of the freezer for a minimum of 10 minutes, ensuring its transformation into a vessel of icy perfection.

2. Within the confines of a cocktail shaker brimming with ice, harmoniously unite the essence of the rose- and elderflower-infused gin, the nectar of freshly squeezed lemon juice, and the golden elixir of honey ginger simple syrup.

3. With an air of determination, vigorously shake the cocktail shaker for 15 to 20 seconds, bestowing upon the ingredients a thorough and enchanting chill as they intertwine in a symphony of flavors.

4. With grace and precision, strain the captivating concoction into the awaiting embrace of the chilled glass, allowing its essence to be captured within its crystalline confines. Add an ice sphere if you wish.

5. With a gentle touch, pour the effervescent elixir of champagne into the glass, delicately crowning the libation with a touch of elegance and a shimmering cascade of bubbles, elevating its allure to new heights.

The Bargain

Gin and Grape Fizz

✦ Makes 1 drink ✦

This enchanting drink is inspired by the fateful agreement struck between a faerie and the chosen one, sealing the latter's destiny with a lifesaving promise and a mystical tattoo. The vibrant hue of Empress 1908 Indigo Gin mirrors the new swirls of ink on her skin. Champagne adds a touch of effervescence, the sparkling bubbles dancing on the palate to echo the whorls of the intricate pattern that now adorns her left forearm and hand, a constant reminder of the price she paid. With each sip you feel the mental tug of a dark shadow watching your every move, waiting until it is time for him to call upon you to fulfill the bargain that was made.

Inspired by *A Court of Thorns and Roses* by Sarah J. Maas (Chapter 37)

1½ ounces Empress 1908 Indigo Gin
2 ounces concord grape juice
1 ounce blue curaçao

Edible glitter (optional)
2 ounces champagne

1. Start with the gin, grape juice, and blue curaçao in a cocktail shaker.

2. Fill the shaker with ice, seal the shaker, and shake it.

3. Choose a tall, elegant flute or a martini glass, something that complements the beauty of your creation. Add an ice sphere to represents the eye watching you.

4. If desired, add a pinch of edible glitter to mimic the stars in his eyes. Strain the mixed potion into your prepared glass.

5. Slowly top off your cocktail with the chilled champagne. The twirling effervescence represents the intricacies of her tattoo.

6. Serve immediately to be best captivated by the cocktail's allure.

A Court
of Tequila

Spicy-Nes

Spicy Jalapeño Margarita

✦ Makes 1 drink ✦

This peppery beverage may be consumed while recuperating from a scolding by a sharp-tongued witch, whose demeanor can be both icy and strategic. Do not allow her curt disposition to mislead you, for she ardently adores and safeguards those she holds dear. When she is not unleashing her verbal prowess upon a valiant warrior, she can be found devouring smut or clinging to a resplendent headboard . . .

Inspired by *A Court of Silver Flames* by Sarah J. Maas (Chapter 41)

2 ounces blanco tequila
1 ounce Cointreau or triple sec (more if you like sweeter)
3 or 4 slices jalapeño

½ lime, cut in wedges
2 ounces fresh lime juice
Tajín or salt for rim
4 ounces limeade

1. Combine the tequila, Cointreau, jalapeño slices (seeds removed for the faint-hearted), two lime wedges, and lime juice into a cocktail shaker.

2. Muddle the components in the shaker.

3. Add a handful of ice into the shaker.

4. Vigorously shake the mixture with determination.

5. Glide a lime wedge along the rim of the glass, dip the glass in Tajín, and fill it with ice.

6. Strain the contents of the shaker into the rimmed glass.

7. Finish it off with limeade and gently stir to perfection.

Night Court

Blackberry Margarita

✦ Makes 1 drink ✦

Step into the enchanting world of the Night Court, where shadows and secrets intertwine with ethereal beauty. This blackberry margarita perfectly captures the dueling essence of the court—one part filled with nightmares, the other a haven of dreams. The deep purple color, infused with the bold flavor of blackberries, mirrors the breathtaking nights that illuminate the Night Court's skies. With each sip you'll experience a delightful blend of tartness and sweetness, a reflection of the intricate balance between light and dark in this mystical realm.

Inspired by *A Court of Thorns and Roses* by Sarah J. Maas (Chapter 24)

2 lime wedges
Coarse salt or sugar for rim
5 or 6 fresh blackberries, more for
  garnish
2 ounces blackberry-infused silver
  tequila (see Infused Alcohol,
  page 140)

1 ounce fresh lime juice
¾ ounce triple sec
Limeade to top
½ ounce lime simple syrup (see Simple
  Syrup, page 136), adjust to taste

1. If rimming the glass, moisten the rim with a lime wedge and dip it into coarse salt. Set aside.

2. In a shaker, muddle the fresh blackberries to release their juices.

3. Add the tequila, lime juice, triple sec, limeade, and simple syrup to the shaker.

4. Fill the shaker with ice and shake vigorously for 15 to 20 seconds.

5. Strain the mixture into the prepared glass filled with ice.

6. Garnish with skewered blackberries and a lime wedge.

Traitor's Tears

Lilac Margarita

✦ Makes 1 drink ✦

Beneath the serene facade of the Spring Court lies a tempestuous force, a whirlwind of raw emotion that can shatter even the strongest of masks. Enter the realm of the Traitor's Tears, a lilac margarita that captures the explosive fury of the High Lord's anguish. The burst of flavor is like emotional shrapnel shattering through the tranquility. Furniture explodes, windows shatter, and the very air trembles with the force of the High Lord's unleashed power, echoed in the tangy bite of this potent concoction. Let the lilac petals and tangy citrus transport you to the heart of this tempestuous tale, where love and loss intertwine in a heady, intoxicating embrace.

Inspired by *A Court of Mist and Fury* by Sarah J. Maas (Chapter 64)

1 lime wedge
Salt or sugar for rim
2 ounces silver tequila
2 ounces fresh lime juice
1 ounce Cointreau

½ ounce lilac or lavender simple syrup
   (see Simple Syrup, page 136)
Lilac blossom or lavender sprig
   for garnish

1. Glide a lime wedge along the edge of a frosted margarita or cocktail glass to dampen it.

2. Submerge the rim into a platter of salt or sugar to craft a salted or sugared edge.

3. Blend the tequila, lime juice, Cointreau, and lilac syrup in a cocktail shaker with ice.

4. Agitate vigorously for 10 to 15 seconds, until impeccably chilled.

5. Pour into the readied rimmed glass.

6. Adorn with a lilac blossom or lavender sprig.

Curse Breaker

Raspberry Passion Fruit Tequila Sour

✦ Makes 1 drink ✦

In a realm shrouded by a dark queen's curse, a brave young heroine is faced with a challenge, and the riddle is the last trial of her fate. Blanco tequila sets the stage for tangy passion fruit and vibrant raspberry, unveiling layers like unraveling the riddle's threads. Bright lemon balances tart and sweet, reflecting the heroine's resolve. Armed with her wit and unwavering determination, she faces a seemingly impossible riddle—to which the answer is "love." This cocktail takes you along for the twists and turns and a life brought back with immense power and appreciation for the one who saved them all and broke the curse.

Inspired by *A Court of Thorns and Roses* by Sarah J. Maas (Chapter 32)

2 ounces blanco tequila
1 ounce fresh lemon juice
1 ounce passion fruit puree

1 ounce raspberry liqueur
3 raspberries

1. Prepare a cocktail shaker by filling it with a generous number of ice cubes.

2. Combine the smooth blanco tequila, lemon juice, luxurious passion fruit puree, and decadent raspberry liqueur in the shaker.

3. Shake with great enthusiasm for 10 to 15 seconds, ensuring a perfectly chilled concoction.

4. Carefully strain the elixir into a frosty cocktail glass, ready to be savored.

5. Adorn the masterpiece with the plump, fresh raspberries elegantly presented either on a cocktail pick or delicately arranged around the rim of the glass.

6. Accept your fate as you sip following your triumphant victory in the ultimate test of intellect.

A Court
of Bubbles

Sparkling Mortals

Grapefruit Mimosa

✦ Makes 1 drink ✦

This cocktail is like the unbreakable bond of three seafaring women. At its base, the tangy and vibrant flavor of grapefruit juice embodies the women's courage and resilience, their spirited determination to face whatever challenges lie ahead. Each element in this drink serves a distinct purpose: The sugar cube embodies the essence of sweetness for a gentle sister, the bitters symbolize a sister with a cutting wit, and the champagne epitomizes a sister who saves them all. Each sip is a testament to their shared strength.

1 dash of bitters
1 sugar cube
Champagne or sparkling wine

Splash of fresh grapefruit juice
Grapefruit slice for garnish
Fresh mint sprig for garnish

1. Sprinkle the bitters over the sugar cube delicately.

2. Position the sugar cube elegantly at the base of your most cherished champagne flute.

3. Pour champagne into the glass, filling it up to three-quarters of the way.

4. Complete the drink by adding grapefruit juice to the top.

5. Adorn the cocktail with a slice of grapefruit and a sprig of fresh mint for a touch of sophistication.

Mistress of Midnight

Raspberry Prosecco Martini

✦ Makes 1 drink ✦

A respite for weary rulers, this elixir balances the bite of raspberry vodka with the coolness of an icy whisper. Sip it slowly, for within its depths lies a secret: It unravels tongues, loosens truths, and transforms enemies into unwitting allies.

Handful of fresh raspberries
½ ounce lime simple syrup (see Simple
   Syrup, page 136)
1½ ounces raspberry vodka
½ ounce fresh lime juice
Prosecco or sparkling wine

Raspberry or lime twist for garnish
1 teaspoon sugar
Dried lime or hollowed-out lime half
   for flames
1 teaspoon 151 rum

1. Blend together the raspberries and sweet simple syrup until smooth, then strain and pour into a cocktail shaker.

2. Mix in the raspberry-infused vodka and zesty lime juice for a tantalizing twist.

3. Fill the shaker with ice and shake energetically for 15 to 20 seconds to chill and blend the flavors.

4. Strain the luscious concoction into a frosty martini glass.

5. Finish the cocktail with a splash of chilled prosecco for a touch of effervescence.

6. Adorn with a vibrant raspberry or lime twist for an alluring presentation.

7. For a fire garnish, pour the sugar in a small pile onto a dried lime. Place the lime gently so it is floating on top of the cocktail. Pour the 151 rum onto the lime. Light the sugar and rum with a lighter. Let it burn out before consuming.

8. Sip while pulling truths from your enemies.

Stardust Spritz

Sparkling Gin and Champagne

✦ Makes 1 drink ✦

A celestial elixir that mirrors the night sky of falling stars. Crafted from gin and blue curaçao, it sparkles like stardust, inviting dreamers to gaze upward and witness meteors migrating through the stars. As these glittering shooting stars find themselves Earthside, they leave their sparkle on any being they touch. Raise your glass, for in every sip lies a whisper of magic and a promise of wonder.

1 ounce gin
½ ounce blue curaçao
½ ounce fresh lemon juice
Fresh lemon slice

Edible star sprinkles
1 pinch silver edible glitter
4 ounces champagne, chilled

1. Combine the gin, blue curaçao, and lemon juice in a mixing glass filled with ice, then gently stir until perfectly chilled.

2. Glide the lemon slice along the rim of the glass. Delicately sprinkle with edible star sprinkles and shimmering edible glitter for a touch of elegance.

3. Carefully strain the mixture into a glass and elegantly top it off with champagne.

4. Envision yourself being wrapped in a mesmerizing dance of celestial stardust gracefully swirling and twirling around you. Envelop yourself in the sheer delight.

Golden Dawn

Orange and Passion Fruit Mimosa

✦ Makes 1 drink ✦

This glowing drink captures the essence of a cobalt sky tinged with the soft remnants of dawn, where golden light edges the clouds and the air is imbued with the dewy freshness of an eternal summer countryside. The sparkling rosé wine provides a delicate, effervescent base, symbolizing the gilded light of dawn that illuminates the lush landscape. Each sip is a refreshing journey through the red-roofed villages and sparkling rivers of this enchanting territory, where every moment is bathed in the gentle glow of the rising sun.

Inspired by *A Court of Wings and Ruin* by Sarah J. Maas (Chapter 42)

Orange juice puree or syrup   **Sparkling rosé wine**
Passion fruit juice puree or syrup

1. In a small pitcher or bowl, combine equal parts orange juice and passion fruit puree. Mix well to blend the flavors.

2. Pour the juice mixture into ice sphere molds, filling each compartment.

3. Freeze the molds for several hours or overnight, until completely solid.

4. Choose an elegant coupe or wine glass to serve your mimosa.

5. Carefully remove the frozen juice spheres from the molds. Place one frozen sphere into the glass.

6. Slowly pour the chilled sparkling rosé wine over the frozen sphere. Pour gently to preserve the bubbles.

7. Serve immediately, allowing the beautiful frozen sphere to slowly infuse the mimosa with the vibrant flavors of orange and passion fruit as it melts, adding a touch of visual and sensory delight.

Faerie Wine

Sparkling Lemonade and Elderflower

✦ Makes 1 drink ✦

Lose your inhibitions with this exquisite elixir that captures the very essence of the fabled faerie wine, renowned for its ability to evoke euphoria and a sense of enchanting liberation. Crafted with elderflower liqueur at its core, this potion exudes a subtle floral sweetness that mirrors the ethereal beauty and captivating charm of the faerie realm. Relish the seamless blend of elderflower, lemonade, and champagne, and surrender to the euphoria and liberation that only faerie wine can bestow.

1 ounce lemonade
½ ounce St-Germaine Elderflower Liqueur

Champagne or sparkling wine

1. In a chilled champagne flute or a sophisticated wine glass, pour the crisp, refreshing lemonade.

2. Gently drizzle in the elderflower liqueur.

3. Slowly top off your creation with chilled champagne. Pour with care, allowing the bubbles to rise gracefully, mingling with the lemonade and elderflower liqueur to create a symphony of flavors.

4. Serve immediately, watching as the sparkling bubbles dance and the aromas captivate.

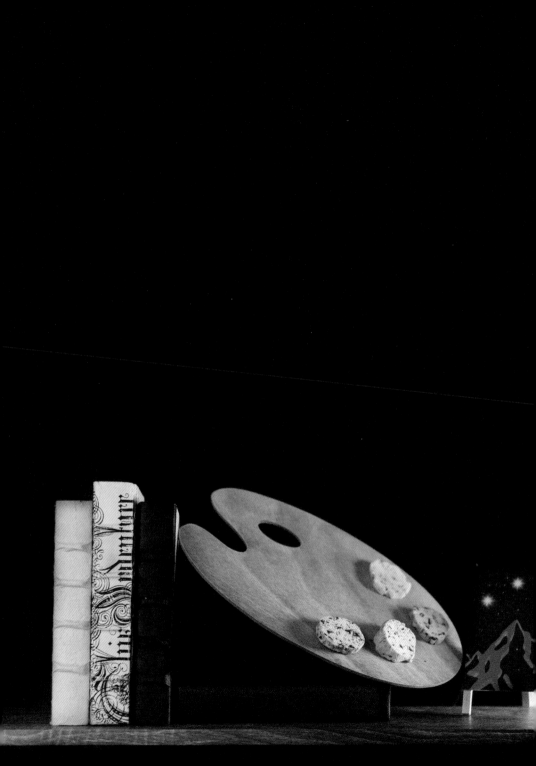

A Court of Appetizers

Bone to Pick

French Bread

✦ **Makes 4 small loaves** ✦

Descend into the chthonic realm, where an ancient, immortal being holds dominion over the mysteries of death itself. In this dark, otherworldly dimension, a loaf of crusty French bread takes on an entirely new form, a sinister yet alluring offering to appease the appetite of a dreaded monster. Each slice reveals a soft, airy interior, the very embodiment of the fragile line between life and the great beyond. As you tear into the bread, the shatteringly crisp crust crackles like the ominous sounds of deep castle dungeons. Embrace the darkness that dwells within its crusty depths, and perhaps, just perhaps, you'll catch a fleeting glimpse of the future that awaits.

3 cups all-purpose flour	**2 teaspoons salt**
1½ cups warm water	**2 teaspoons active dry yeast**

1. Add all the ingredients into a mixing bowl.

2. Stir until combined; it will be sticky.

3. Cover with a kitchen towel and let rise for 90 minutes.

4. Transfer the dough to a lightly floured surface and fold it in on itself to form a smooth ball.

5. Cut in four equal parts.

6. Preheat oven to 475°F.

7. Cover a baking sheet with parchment paper and lightly dust with flour.

8. Form each dough piece into a 10-inch-long, smooth log by taking its edges and pinching them together.

continues

9. Place the dough logs seam down on a baking sheet.

10. Cover with a kitchen towel and let rise for 30 minutes.

11. Once the dough has risen, take a razor or sharp knife and slash the top of each baguette at a 30-degree angle in three places.

12. Place an ovenproof dish of water on the top rack in the oven.

13. Place the baking sheet of baguettes into the oven on the bottom rack.

14. Bake for 30 minutes, or until crusty and golden.

Cauldron Fondue

Cheese Fondue

✦ Makes 10 servings ✦

Within the hallowed depths of an ancient cauldron, a primordial force simmers, a bubbling potion that controls life and death. Dip into the fondue's creamy depths to discover a harmonious blend of savory and nutty flavors, each one a distinct thread woven into the tapestry of fate. The sharp bite of aged cheddar mingles with the earthy notes of Gruyère, adding a delicate counterpoint and mirroring the intricate balance that governs the universe's grand design.

1 garlic clove, cut in half
1 cup dry white wine (such as
    sauvignon blanc or pinot grigio)
1 tablespoon fresh lemon juice
1 cup sharp cheddar cheese, grated
1 cup Gruyère cheese, grated

1 tablespoon cornstarch
Freshly ground black pepper to taste
Green apples, French bread (see page
    111), and blanched vegetables (such
    as broccoli, cauliflower, and carrots)
    for dipping

1. Rub the inside of your fondue pot with the cut sides of the garlic halves. Discard the garlic after use.

2. Pour the white wine into the fondue pot and heat over medium heat until it is just starting to simmer. Do not let it boil.

3. Stir in the lemon juice. This helps to stabilize the cheese and prevents it from becoming stringy.

4. In a large bowl, toss the grated sharp cheddar and Gruyère cheeses with the cornstarch. The cornstarch will help to thicken the fondue and prevent clumping.

continues

5. Gradually add the cheese to the simmering wine, a handful at a time, stirring constantly with a wooden spoon or spatula. Ensure each handful is melted before adding more cheese.

6. Season the fondue with the black pepper.

7. Keep the fondue warm over low heat. If your fondue pot has a heating element or is designed to be used with a small burner, now is the time to utilize it.

8. Serve immediately with an assortment of dippers, such as cubed crusty bread, blanched vegetables, and apple slices.

TIPS: If the fondue is too thick, add a little more wine. If it's too thin, add more cheese. Ensure your dippers are prepped and ready before starting the fondue to enjoy the cheese at its best texture and flavor.

Stir the fondue in a figure-eight motion to help keep it smooth and prevent it from clumping.

Inner Circle

Deviled Eggs with Chimichurri and Prosciutto

✦ Makes 24 eggs ✦

Step into the Court of Dreams, a realm where the veil between slumber and waking life grows gossamer-thin, and behold the Inner Circle. This fine assembly of deviled eggs, crowned with vibrant chimichurri and delicate ribbons of prosciutto, pays homage to the High Lord's trusted coterie, the dreamers who help govern the ethereal realms of the Night Court.

Inspired by *A Court of Mist and Fury* by Sarah J. Maas (Chapter 16)

Deviled Eggs
12 eggs
½ cup mayonnaise
1 tablespoon stone-ground mustard
1 teaspoon red wine vinegar
1 teaspoon garlic powder
½ teaspoon onion powder
½ teaspoon paprika
Salt and pepper to taste
Prosciutto for garnish

Chimichurri
½ cup fresh flat-leaf parsley
¼ cup fresh cilantro
¼ cup fresh chives
¼ cup extra virgin olive oil
3 garlic cloves
½ fresh shallot
1 tablespoon red wine vinegar or white wine vinegar
Salt and pepper to taste

1. Place the eggs in a single layer in a saucepan and cover with enough water to come at least an inch above the eggs.

2. Bring the water to a rolling boil over high heat. Once the water is boiling, cover the saucepan and remove it from heat. Let the eggs sit in the hot water for 12 minutes.

3. After 12 minutes, transfer the eggs to a bowl of ice water to cool completely. This stops the cooking process and makes them easier to peel.

continues

4. Once the eggs are cooled, gently tap them on a hard surface to crack the shells. Peel the eggs under running water to help remove the shells cleanly.

5. Slice the eggs in half lengthwise and carefully remove the yolks. Place the yolks in a medium bowl and the whites on a serving platter.

6. Mash the yolks with a fork until they are completely crumbled.

7. Add the mayonnaise, mustard, red wine vinegar, garlic powder, onion powder, paprika, salt, and pepper to the mashed yolks. Mix until smooth and creamy. Adjust the seasoning to taste.

8. Use a spoon or a piping bag fitted with a star tip to fill the egg white halves with the yolk mixture. If you don't have a piping bag, you can use a plastic sandwich bag with a corner snipped off.

9. Arrange the deviled eggs on a serving platter and refrigerate while you make your chimichurri.

10. For your chimichurri, add all the ingredients into a food processor and pulse until everything is finely chopped and combined. Season to taste.

11. Thinly slice the prosciutto into ribbons and roll each ribbon into a small rose or ball shape.

12. When ready to serve, spoon about ½ teaspoon of chimichurri mixture on each egg.

13. Place the prosciutto on top of each egg and serve.

Painter's Palette

Compound Butter Board

✦ Makes 1 cup of each butter ✦

Here we have a canvas of flavors waiting to stroke your senses: roasted garlic, sun-dried tomatoes, red wine, and chipotle. Crusty bread swiftly glides through the colored butters like a paint brush—each swipe a revelation; each bite a masterpiece. Will you adorn your slice with swirls of rosemary, or perhaps trace the contours of your lover's lips? The choice, dear reader, is yours to savor and create. Serve with a baguette or breadsticks.

For the Garlic Herb Butter
1 cup butter
1 head garlic
Olive oil
Salt to taste
2 tablespoons chives, finely chopped
1 tablespoon parsley, finely chopped
1 tablespoon rosemary, finely chopped
Cracked black pepper to taste

For the Red Wine and Shallot Butter
1 cup butter
¼ cup red wine
1 clove garlic, minced
1 shallot, finely chopped
1 bunch parsley, finely chopped
Flaky sea salt and cracked black
    pepper to taste

For the Sun-Dried Tomato Butter
1 cup butter
¼ cup sun-dried tomatoes, finely
    chopped
1 tablespoon fresh basil, finely chopped
1 to 2 garlic cloves, minced
Flaky sea salt and cracked black
    pepper to taste

For the Chipotle Lime Compound Butter
1 cup butter
3 chipotle peppers in adobo
    sauce, minced
1 tablespoon fresh lime juice
2 garlic cloves, minced
Flaky sea salt and cracked black
    pepper to taste

continues

1. Place all 4 cups of butter on the counter until it is soft and room temperature.

2. For the garlic herb butter, first roast the garlic. Cut about ¼ to ½ inch off the top of the head of garlic, exposing the tops of the cloves.

3. Place the garlic head on a piece of aluminum foil and wrap it, leaving the top exposed.

4. Drizzle each garlic head generously with olive oil, making sure to cover all the exposed cloves.

5. Sprinkle with a pinch of salt.

6. Place the garlic in a preheated oven on 400°F and roast for 40 to 45 minutes, or until the cloves are tender and golden brown. The exact time can vary depending on the size of the garlic head.

7. In the meantime, for the red wine and shallot butter, place the wine and chopped shallot in a saucepan, bring to a boil, and reduce down until almost no wine is left, 5 to 10 minutes.

8. Set aside and cool.

9. Now it is time to assemble your butter mixtures. To do so, get four medium bowls. To each bowl add 1 cup softened butter.

10. For the roasted garlic butter, make sure the roasted garlic is cooled, then squeeze it into the butter. Add the chopped chives, parsley, and rosemary, salt, and pepper to taste into the bowl of softened butter.

11. For the red wine and shallot butter, add the cooled red wine and shallot reduction to the butter. Add the minced garlic, chopped parsley, salt, and pepper to taste into the bowl of softened butter.

12. For the sun-dried tomato butter, add the chopped sun-dried tomatoes, basil, minced garlic, salt, and pepper to taste into the bowl of softened butter.

13. For the chipotle lime butter, add the minced peppers, lime juice, minced garlic, salt, and pepper to taste into the bowl of softened butter.

continues

14. Mix the ingredients in each bowl.

15. Lay out four pieces of cling wrap on the counter. Put each batch of butter on its own piece of cling wrap.

16. Roll and wrap the butter in the cling wrap, making a log shape about 2 inches in diameter.

17. Roll as tightly as possible and tie knots at the ends of each butter log.

18. Place in the refrigerator for 2 hours to chill.

Potato Rations

Potato Rounds with Cheese and Jalapeño Ranch

✦ Makes 24 rounds ✦

In the wake of fortune's cruel betrayal, a family once accustomed to opulence found themselves humbled, their great wealth stripped away, leaving only the barest of rations to sustain them. These unassuming discs, crafted from the simplest of ingredients, belie a depth of flavor that defies their modest origins. The crisp, golden potato rounds form the foundation, their earthy essence a testament to the nourishing bounty of the land itself. Each bite yields a satisfying crunch, transporting you to simpler times when the most basic pleasures were savored and cherished.

For the Jalapeño Ranch
4 tablespoons sour cream
2 tablespoons mayonnaise
1 tablespoon minced pickles
1 tablespoon fresh jalapeño, seeded and minced
1 teaspoon pickle juice
1 teaspoon buttermilk
¼ teaspoon garlic powder
¼ teaspoon onion powder
¼ teaspoon parsley
¼ teaspoon black pepper

For the Potato Rounds
3 russet potatoes
Olive oil for brushing
½ cup sharp cheddar cheese, shredded
Green onion, chopped
Bacon bits

1. For the jalapeño ranch, add all the ingredients in a bowl, mix together, and place in the refrigerator for at least 30 minutes to combine flavors.

2. Preheat oven to 350°F.

3. For the potato rounds, begin by washing the potatoes and slicing into thin rounds (about ¼ inch thick).

continues

4. Place the potatoes in a pot filled with water and bring to a boil. Cook for 3 to 4 minutes. Drain and pat dry the potatoes.

5. Place foil on a baking pan and spray with cooking spray. Place the potatoes on the pan. Brush lightly with olive oil.

6. Bake for 12 to 14 minutes, until brown.

7. Sprinkle each round with shredded cheese and put back into the oven until the cheese is melted.

8. Once melted, place the rounds on a serving tray. Put 1 teaspoon of ranch on each potato round.

9. Sprinkle the potatoes with green onions and bacon bits, then serve.

Tavern Sausage Rolls

Sausage and Puff Pastry

✦ Makes 54 rolls ✦

Step into the cozy confines of a humble tavern nestled in the heart of the mortal lands, where the scents of hearth and home mingle with the laughter and camaraderie of weary travelers. Here, amid the warm glow of flickering lanterns and the clink of well-worn mugs, you'll find a taste of true comfort. Golden, flaky pastry encases a succulent filling of seasoned pork sausage, its rich, herbaceous aroma wafting through the tavern like a siren's call to the hungry and homesick alike.

1 pound mild Italian ground sausage	**1 teaspoon garlic powder**
1 pound ground turkey	**Pinch salt and pepper**
2 tablespoons sweet chili sauce	**17 ounces puff pastry sheets**
1 cup sharp cheddar cheese, shredded	**1 egg**

1. Preheat oven to 400°F.

2. In a large bowl, combine the ground sausage, ground turkey, sweet chili sauce, shredded cheese, garlic powder, salt, and pepper. Mix until fully combined.

3. Roll out puff pastry into two 11-by-12.5-inch rectangles, about ⅛ inch thick. Cut each sheet into thirds, about 4 inches wide. Roll the meat mixture into a long log, about 1 inch wide, and place in the center of each piece of pastry.

4. Fold the pastry over the top of the meat log on each side and apply pressure to secure the seams and ensure meat is fully wrapped.

5. Cut each log into 1-inch pieces, approximately 9 small rolls. Place each piece seam side down on a parchment paper–lined baking sheet.

6. Brush the top of each roll with the egg mixture.

7. Bake for 25 to 30 minutes, until golden and cooked through.

Riverside Smokies

Bacon-Wrapped Smokies with Brown Sugar Glaze

✦ Makes 27 servings ✦

Nestled along the banks of the winding Sidra River, you notice an inviting glow that casts a golden hue upon the gently rippling waters. Enter these bite-sized morsels of smoked sausage lovingly enrobed in sweet, caramelized bacon. Each smoky nugget glistens under a supple glaze of brown sugar, its deep, savory notes mingling with the bacon's salty-sweet allure in a tantalizing dance upon the tongue. Each bite is a celebration of the simple pleasures, a reminder that even in the most unassuming corners of the world, magic can be found in the form of a perfectly executed dish.

Inspired by *A Court of Mist and Fury* by Sarah J. Maas (Chapter 15)

1 pound bacon (the thinner the better)
1 pack (approximately 27 in a pack)
   Hillshire Farms Lit'l Smokies,
   original or beef

Toothpicks
Brown sugar

1. Preheat oven to 400°F.

2. Cut the bacon lengthwise, then cut each strip in half at the middle point to create four bacon ribbons from 1 piece of bacon.

3. Wrap each smokie with a piece of bacon and secure with a toothpick.

4. Roll the smokie in brown sugar.

5. Line a baking tray with aluminum foil and spray with nonstick cooking spray.

6. Place the bacon-wrapped smokies on the baking tray.

7. Bake the smokies for 30 to 45 minutes, flipping halfway, until brown.

Gambling Chips

Kettle Chips, Melted Gorgonzola with Balsamic Drizzle

✦ Makes 13 servings ✦

Step into the dimly lit, sultry atmosphere of the hamlet's tavern, where the air thrums with the pulsing beat of music and the tantalizing clink of chips upon the gambling tables. These crispy, golden discs are the perfect accompaniment to a night of high stakes and even higher spirits. Each bite unleashes a burst of flavor that dances across the palate like the skilled footwork of the patrons as they twirl and sway to the rhythm of the tavern's thumping bass line.

Salted kettle-style potato chips   **Camembert or Brie cheese**
Gorgonzola cheese   **Balsamic glaze**

1. Line a baking tray with parchment paper.

2. Evenly distribute the chips in a single layer on the tray.

3. Crumble the cheeses with your hands over the chips, ensuring every chip has both cheeses on it.

4. Put the tray in the oven on the top rack and turn on broil to toast the chips. Keep an eye on the chips, as some broilers can be stronger than others and burn food quickly.

5. The chips are finished when the cheese is melty and the chips are golden.

6. Drizzle with the balsamic glaze and serve.

Smutty Bites

Sautéed Dates with Rosemary and Crushed Pistachios

✦ Makes 12 to 15 bites ✦

Prepare to surrender your senses to the sultry allure of these bites, where decadence and desire intertwine in a tantalizing embrace. As you gaze upon these succulent morsels, their plump, glistening forms beckon you closer, tempting you to succumb to their seductive charms. Inhale deeply so that the intoxicating aroma of rosemary envelops you as the subtle heat of the herbs dances across your palate, igniting a slow burn that smolders within and builds with delicious anticipation. These delectable treats are most pleasurable when savored while you nestle upon a sumptuous sofa, accompanied by a cherished smutty novel that ignites the flames of desire within.

2 tablespoons unsalted butter or
   olive oil
2 or 3 fresh rosemary sprigs,
   finely chopped

12 to 15 large Medjool dates, pitted
¼ cup shelled pistachios, crushed
Pinch of sea salt (optional, to taste)

1. In a skillet or frying pan, melt butter (or olive oil to make it vegan) over medium heat.

2. Once the butter is melted and the skillet is heated, add the chopped rosemary to the pan. Sauté for about 1 minute to infuse the butter with the rosemary flavor.

3. Add the pitted dates to the skillet, arranging them in a single layer. Cook undisturbed for 2 to 3 minutes, until they begin to caramelize and soften.

4. Gently flip the dates with a spatula to ensure even cooking. Sauté for an additional 2 to 3 minutes, until the dates are caramelized and tender.

5. Transfer the sautéed dates to a serving platter and sprinkle generously with crushed pistachios.

6. To enhance flavors and provide a delightful contrast, add a pinch of sea salt to each date.

A Court
of Syrups
and Infusions

Simple Syrup

✦ Makes 1 cup ✦

Elevate your cocktails with these flavor-forward syrups. Refreshing and indulgent, they awaken the senses. Infusion ingredients from the recipes include lime, rosemary, rose, brown sugar, honey, ginger, and lilac or lavender.

1 cup sugar
1 cup water

2 tablespoons of the ingredient(s) of your choice (optional, if infusing)

1. In a medium pan, heat the sugar and water on a stovetop.

2. Bring to a light boil while stirring and reduce the heat.

3. Add the desired infusion and let simmer for 10 to 15 minutes, until all the sugar has dissolved and it has a syrup consistency. Remove from the heat and let cool.

4. Strain out the infusion ingredient and pour the syrup into an airtight container and refrigerate.

 NOTE: For honey syrups, which are also rich and delicious, replace the sugar with honey at the same 1:1 ratio.

Blackberry Liqueur

✦ Makes 1 cup ✦

This rich and luscious liqueur is crafted from blackberries, robust red wine, pure cane sugar, and a touch of vodka. This exquisite liqueur is a celebration of the vibrant flavors of summer, which are captured in every sip, offering a symphony of sweetness, depth, and sophistication that mirrors the sultry seduction of your favorite mythic man.

1 cup red wine
½ cup blackberries

2 teaspoons sugar
1 ounce vodka

1. Add the wine and blackberries to a container.

2. Muddle the berries.

3. Put on a lid and leave for 48 hours.

4. Strain the liquid and add it to a pot over medium heat.

5. Add the sugar and simmer for 10 to 15 minutes.

6. Remove from the heat, add the vodka, and cool.

7. Store refrigerated.

Infused Alcohol

✦ Makes one 750 ml bottle ✦

You can create a decadent collection of infused alcohols, where spirits are transformed into captivating elixirs infused with the finest botanicals, fruits, herbs, and spices. Recipes throughout this book include garlic-, blueberry-, and blackberry-infused spirits. Crafted with ingredients to elevate any cocktail, each bottle is a celebration of flavor, aroma, and innovation.

1 to 2 cups of flavorings for infusion (if using berries, use frozen)	**750 ml bottle of your choice of alcohol (vodka, gin, rum, tequila, whiskey)**

1. Place the flavorings into a clean airtight glass container, such as a mason jar.

2. Pour the alcohol over the ingredients, making sure they are fully submerged.

3. Seal the container tightly with the lid.

4. Store the container in a cool, dark place. Shake it gently once a day to help distribute the flavors.

5. Let sit for 2 to 3 days (or more for fruits). Sample to see if ready.

6. Once the infusion reaches the desired flavor, strain the alcohol through a fine mesh sieve or cheesecloth into a clean glass bottle or jar to remove the solid ingredients.

7. Seal the bottle and label it with the date and type of infusion. Enjoy!

8. Store your infused alcohol in a cool, dark place. Most infusions can be kept for up to a year.

Index